ational

iams

I'm going to commend this book to everyone in my church family. Why? Because I love Paul Williams' pastoral heart. When it comes to telling others about the Lord Jesus Christ, he knows people have fears and addresses those fears. I love his methodology. He insists the best answers come from the lips of Jesus and I love the fact he models reaching out to others.

RICO TICE, SENIOR MINISTER, ALL SOULS CHURCH & CHRISTIANITY EXPLORED

'Real life conversations are messy,' says Paul Williams – how true! This engaging book will equip you to navigate such conversations and clearly share your faith in Jesus Christ. You will find challenge, encouragement and inspiration on every page. I love this book!

REVD CANON MICK WOODHEAD, TEAM RECTOR, STC SHEFFIELD

This book deals beautifully with the fear of evangelism by enabling the reader to see that it's possible to be on the 'front foot' when sharing the gospel. His encouragement to keep our focus on what Jesus says as opposed to more abstract debating points is terrific, as is his reminder that if someone asks questions we do best by reciprocating with questions so that we can engage in a conversation, not defend a position. Finally, he takes all the pressure off us by clarifying that it is God's role to open people's eyes and ours to pray for opportunities for conversations with the right people. A really great read for anyone nervous about evangelism!

GRAHAM DANIELS, CHRISTIANS IN SPORT

Intentional

Evangelism That Takes People to Jesus

Paul Williams

www.uniontheology.org

a division of 10ofthose.com

Copyright © 2016 by Paul Williams

First published in Great Britain in 2016

British Library Cataloguing in Publication Data
A record for this book is available from the British Library

ISBN: 978-1-910587-52-2

Designed by Steve Devane

Printed in the UK by CPI Group (UK) Ltd, Croydon, CR0 4YY

10Publishing, a division of 10ofthose.com
Unit C, Tomlinson Road, Leyland, PR25 2DY, England
Email: info@10ofthose.com

Website: www.10ofthose.com

Dedication

For Bernard, whose infectious passion for sharing
Jesus with everyone is an inspiration to me.
For Paul, who first introduced me to the idea
of taking people to Jesus when answering any
question.
With thanks to Julia, without whose
encouragement and support this book would
never have been written.

CONTENTS

Nothing more important

'I know there's nothing more important in the world, but I just don't know where to start.' Kate had been a Christian some months and had tried her best to tell her friends and family about Jesus, but she felt she wasn't getting anywhere.

'I know exactly what you mean,' I said. Because I did. I found becoming a Christian so thrilling. Being forgiven! Having eternal life! Knowing Jesus Christ! It really was the best news I'd ever heard. Still is. The morning after I turned to Christ, it was as if everything in the world was sweeter. The birds' song was more tuneful. The colours on the trees, more vivid. The cool breeze on my face, more refreshing. Even the irritating noise of the neighbours' barking dog was more bearable. Everything had changed. When I went to work the next day, I had a new spring in my step and my heart was bursting with the excitement of the most momentous news about Jesus Christ. I started to tell my colleagues the gospel – as best I could. And I really expected them to want to become Christians – just as I had. I really believed they'd all thank me for telling them this brilliant news. I don't need to tell you that it didn't turn out that way!

So I really did know exactly what Kate meant. I very quickly discovered that people aren't always thrilled to hear about Jesus. Even those who don't laugh in your face have serious questions – deep, important questions. Back then, I hadn't even thought about some of those questions. And those questions I had thought about, I couldn't explain very well.

My guess is that you've had a similar experience. Therefore this book is an attempt to help you, Kate and anyone else who is excited by the greatest news in the entire universe and wants to share it, but who doesn't really know where to begin.

So, let's begin …

Overcoming fear

1

I can remember it as clearly as if it were yesterday – the first time I felt really frightened. I was only six years old and had wandered away from the caravan my family and I were staying in. I can still picture myself standing in a forest, all alone, surrounded by trees and not knowing where to turn with every potential route back looking identical. Disorientated and frightened, I started to shout, 'Mummy, Daddy!' In no time at all the shouting became frantic, terrified screaming and crying. The fact I'm writing this now, forty-seven years later, tells you though that I wasn't lost forever or eaten by a bear – which would have been a quite remarkable end to the story as we were in Dorset at the time!

My parents heard my screams. It seems I'd not wandered very far away at all, and so I was very soon back in the safety of the campsite and licking an ice cream, with the added bonus of a chocolate flake, because I'd been such a brave boy!

Since then, I've experienced fear many times: when I nearly drowned in a local swimming pool; when I was cornered by a vicious dog; when I was about to ski down the black run at the top of Mürren's 9,744 foot Schilthorn; and when I have tried to talk to friends about Jesus Christ. Yes, talking to friends about Jesus engenders fear. When I think about it in the cold light of day, I wonder why I get so fearful. It's not as if I live in a part of the world where trying to proselytise carries the death sentence. Usually I'm not talking to unpredictable strangers with raging tempers. Often I am talking to people I know well – to good friends. These people are not going to punch me on the nose. They're not even likely to give me a verbal tongue-lashing, leaving me publicly humiliated. For sure, some of my friends have strong opinions about 'religion'. They disagree with the things I say about Jesus Christ. But they are still my friends. We debate everything from what the current England football manager should do following another disappointing World Cup, to the way the government is running the country. I join in those debates without feeling any fear whatsoever. But when the conversation turns to Jesus Christ, my heart rate rises, my palms get sweaty and my mouth goes dry. It's a strange thing, but it seems I'm not alone.

Whenever I ask people what most inhibits them from sharing the good news of Jesus Christ with others, the most common answer I hear is 'Fear'. Fear of not knowing what to say. Fear of losing friends. Fear of being ridiculed. Fear of saying the wrong thing and putting people off Christianity. And, if the conversation is at work, the fear of losing a job, or a promotion.

The Bible's answer to fear in evangelism is not complicated. It is to fear God more than people.

The apostle Peter, writing to Christians who were tempted not to speak about Jesus, said:

'Do not fear what they fear; do not be frightened.' But in your hearts set apart Christ as Lord (1 Pet. 3:14–15).

Peter was writing to Christians who were suffering for their faith. These believers were not suffering for doing wrong but because they were Christians. If they just kept their heads down and their mouths shut, they'd have enjoyed a quiet life. But Peter wanted to encourage his readers to stand up and speak out for Jesus, even in the face of considerable opposition. In verse 14 Peter quotes Isaiah chapter 8 – another occasion when the people of God had good reason to fear. Back in Isaiah's day, Judah feared the invasion of a mighty army, but, through the prophet Isaiah, the Lord said to them:

Do not call conspiracy everything that these people call conspiracy; do not fear what they fear, and do not dread it. The LORD Almighty is the one you are to regard as holy, he is the one you are to fear (Is. 8:12–13).

Fear the Lord, says Isaiah. Fear the Lord more than people, even when you have good reason to fear people. The people threatening Judah in Isaiah's day could have done them very real harm. The people of Judah faced death no less. Peter's readers also faced serious threats from unbelievers. Would they give way to fear and keep quiet about their faith in Jesus Christ? To overcome the fear of others, the answer is always to fear the Lord. Or, as Peter put it, we are to 'set apart Christ as Lord'.

The Bible often speaks about fearing the Lord, but it can sound like a strange idea to us. As Christians, surely we no longer fear God's judgment on our sins? That is true. We do not fear God's punishment. But there is another way in which believers should retain a right fear of the Lord.

When my twin daughters were toddlers, they used to love playing a game called 'lions'. The game was very straightforward. Susannah and Bethan would run into another room in the house, I would get on all fours, crawl into the room they were in and roar like a lion. They would then run past me into another room, and I would crawl into that room, roaring again like a lion. The girls loved it. They would giggle and scream with delight, and as the game went on, they would whip themselves into an excitable frenzy. 'Louder, Daddy, louder,' they would shout, wanting me to produce a bigger and bigger 'roar' as I entered the room. On one occasion, with the girls' giggling having turned into uncontrollable laughter and their pleas of 'Louder, Daddy, louder' having become ever more desperate, I got up off my hands and knees, stood up as tall as I could and ran into the next room, letting out the biggest roar I could muster. The girls burst into tears ... and ran towards me, grabbing hold of my legs. Once Mummy had arrived to sort out the 'mess' I'd created and the girls had calmed down, I realised the girls' reaction was a brilliant illustration of what it means to fear the Lord. My girls were genuinely frightened of me as I roared like a lion. They couldn't escape me. I was bigger than them and more powerful than them. But I was also their father. In their fear, they instinctively knew that the safest thing to do was to run to me.

That's what it means to fear the Lord. God is the Almighty Creator of the entire universe. He is to be feared. But he is also our strength, our fortress, our stronghold ... and our Father. Running to him brings us to a place of ultimate security. Being with him is the safest place in the universe. So to overcome our fear of others and what they might do to us, in our hearts we need to fear the Lord, or, as Peter put it, 'set apart Christ as Lord'. That means putting Christ first and above all others. It is being more concerned to please him and live for him than anything or anyone else.

God is the Almighty Creator of the entire universe. He is to be feared

It is running to him for our protection and security.

It is easy for us to lose sight of who really rules the world and the future and every detail of life, especially when unbelievers look impressive and threatening. But it is Christ who is the all-powerful Lord of the universe. Our future is ultimately in his hands, not in the hands of those who oppose us. Christ is the one who controls and protects our eternal destiny. We need to remember how awesome and holy Christ is. In that sense, we need to fear and revere him. He is the Lord we serve. We need to set apart Christ as Lord in our hearts. Christ the Lord is also our loving saviour who laid down his life to save us. We should love him and we should fear displeasing Christ more than displeasing those who oppose us. If we fear the Lord, it changes how we see everything and everyone else. Fear of the Lord is the first step to overcoming fear of others. That applies whether it be the fear of not knowing what to say when we're talking to people about Jesus, or the fear of losing friends, or of being ridiculed. It is true whether we fear losing out on a promotion or losing a job through standing up for Christ. If we were in a different culture, it would also be true even if we were in fear of losing our life.

The three C's

2

It was Sunday night. Greg was walking down Regent Street in London's West End with Tim, who was the friend of a friend of Greg's. As they walked, they were chatting about the sermon they had just heard at church. The discussion had been going for some time when Tim said, 'You know, I'm glad I came along tonight and I enjoyed what the preacher had to say, but I'm still not convinced that Jesus is God. Tell me, why are you a Christian?'

The next morning, as I was having coffee with Greg, he was reflecting on that conversation the night before and what happened next. 'When Tim said that he wasn't a Christian,' Greg recalled, 'at that point I froze. I didn't know what to say. It was the strangest thing. Until then, thinking Tim was a Christian, I'd been talking naturally and easily about Jesus, but as soon as I realised that

Tim wasn't a Christian, I felt completely tongue-tied. Goodness only knows what Tim must have thought of me after that. I could barely string a sentence together.'

Christians tell me they have had opportunities to speak about Jesus only to feel that they've blown it

Perhaps it's because we care so much and because we know it matters so much, but time and again I hear the same thing. Christians tell me they have had opportunities to speak about Jesus only to feel that they've blown it. One person put it like this, 'I get so frustrated with myself. I want to tell people about Jesus, but when the opportunity arises, either I don't open my mouth, or I do and then wish I hadn't!'

A most mild-mannered and gentle girl said to me, 'Whenever people question me about my faith in Jesus, for some reason I get really aggressive. It's like I'm related to the incredible hulk. Suddenly there's an aggressive alter ego trying to get out of me!'

There's a physiological explanation for these reactions. It's the flight or fight response. Biologically, we're wired up so that when we sense danger, the brain releases a hormonal cascade that means we either run away or fight back. That's why for some of us, when we're asked what we believe about Jesus, our bodies may react with an increased heart rate, sweaty palms and a dry mouth – those are the physiological symptoms of fear. It's the reason why some people choose to say nothing (the equivalent of running away – the flight response) but others become aggressive (the fight reaction), turning a delightful girl into an aggressive green monster! It's also why, when writing to Christians who had good reason to fear what might happen to them, the apostle Peter had to remind them that they should answer questions about their faith with 'gentleness and respect' (1 Pet. 3:15). Fear of others might well result in a hostile and scornful response from us.

In chapter 1 we looked at how Peter knew that fear stops Christians from speaking about Christ. We saw that the way to overcome the fear of others is to fear the Lord more, or, as Peter puts it, to 'set apart Christ as Lord' in our hearts. We need to have Christ as Lord if we are going to speak out for him. Knowing Christ as Lord transforms us. It helps us overcome the fight or flight response in a whole range of ways. Here are three. And conveniently they all begin with the letter 'C'.

1. Conviction
The first is conviction – the conviction that Christ's gospel is true.

Having a deep conviction of the truth of the gospel will help us to overcome our fear of speaking out. If we fully believe that there really is no other way for anyone to be saved except in Christ, then how can we keep silent? The deep belief that men and women really are doomed for all eternity, unless they repent and believe the good news, will motivate us to overcome our fears and to speak about Jesus.

Let me confess to you that I need to keep hearing the truth of the gospel because I am always being tempted to revise the gospel, to change the gospel or to believe that the gospel isn't true. Now at this point you may be tempted to put this book down and never to pick it up again, and to wonder why the publisher asked me to write this book, and to pray for the poor people of Christ Church Fulwood who have me as their pastor. But before you close the book, let me explain.

I love playing tennis and I've made some really good friends at the local tennis club. One or two of them now come to church regularly, but most of them don't believe the gospel. But let me tell you, they are really nice people. I have seen them go out of their way in their care and concern of others in the tennis club. So when I think of my friends at the tennis club, and how kind they are, I am regularly tempted to think, 'They're not that bad; they're good people.' But once I start to think like that, it's a very short step to then revising the gospel and thinking, 'They'll be OK when they come face to face with God, won't they?'

The moment I think those thoughts, I won't make any attempt to overcome my fear in evangelism. If I think someone is a good person and that God couldn't possibly judge a decent, moral, law-abiding citizen, then why would I engage in a difficult conversation about Jesus and run the risk of losing a friendship? If kind, respectable people are acceptable to God, then why, at work, would I try and persuade a colleague that Jesus Christ is Lord and chance being overlooked for

> *When I think that people are decent and nice, I have forgotten what the gospel actually teaches me*

the promotion I've worked so hard for, or even run the risk of losing my job? If I'm going to overcome fear in evangelism, I have to be convinced that the gospel is true. When I think that people are decent and nice, I have forgotten what the gospel actually teaches me. I have forgotten what sin is. The heart of sin is the rejection of the living God. Sin is not wanting to give the Lord of the universe his proper place in your life. And my friends, delightful as they are, don't want God controlling their lives. Some won't even accept my invitation to the carol service.

When we know Christ as Lord in our heart, it will lead to a conviction that his gospel is true. If we're going to speak out for Christ, we need to have a clarity about what the gospel is. We need to be persuaded that God wants everyone to hear this gospel. Only when we are deeply convinced about the importance and urgency of the gospel, will we do everything we can to overcome our fears and speak about Jesus.

2. Compassion

Second, we need Christ's compassion.

As we know Christ as Lord, we will increasingly see the world through his eyes. His concerns will become our concerns. We will begin to share his compassion for his lost world. And this compassion will motivate us to tell people about Jesus, even when it costs us.

I began to understand how important this 'C' is a few years ago when I worked with the evangelist Rico Tice. At a midweek lunchtime service, Rico was preaching on Luke chapter 16 – about the rich man and Lazarus. As Rico preached, he painted a vivid picture from the Bible of how terrible hell will be and he said, 'If you believe this, you will tell people.' And I sat there thinking to myself, 'I do believe it.' But I knew that I didn't always grasp every opportunity I had to tell people the good news of Jesus Christ as I should.

Rico continued, 'If you believe this and you don't tell people it can mean only one thing – you don't love them.' That hit me like a ton of bricks. Very often that is the reason I don't tell people about Jesus. It's because I don't care enough for them. I don't love them.

Jesus' view of people is so very different from mine. In Matthew chapter 9, we read:

When he [Jesus] saw the crowds, he had compassion on them, because they were harassed and helpless, like sheep without a shepherd (Mt. 9:36).

But when I look at crowds of people, I am often irritated by them because they are in my way. I'm not moved with compassion for people as Jesus is. When I look at groups of people, I am tempted to think they're sorted because they seem to be perfectly happy with their lot in life. But if I saw people as Jesus sees them, I would have compassion for them – because whatever it looks like, people are not sorted. Even those who seem to be happy and content with life are in mortal danger. Without Christ, they are only a

Even those who seem to be happy and content with life are in mortal danger

breath away from coming face to face with God and spending eternity without him.

It's hard sometimes to have compassion for huge groups of people that we don't know from Adam. But if we share our lives with people, if we make genuine friendships with them and pray for them, we will increasingly grow to love them. Then compassion for them will drive us to overcome our fears and tell them about Jesus.

3. Confidence

A third way to overcome fear is confidence. This too flows from knowing Christ as Lord. There are two kinds of confidence I want to talk about here. First, at a practical level, there is the confidence to know how to answer questions.

So many of the fears we have in evangelism stem from not knowing what to say when we're in a conversation.

I used to work in the newspaper industry. Every morning, before I set off for work, I'd read my Bible and in my prayers I would pray for opportunities to share the gospel with my colleagues at work. I loved my job. It was demanding and full on.

There were many deadlines to hit every week and the market was fiercely competitive. We had exacting targets to reach. In the promotions and marketing department we worked hard together but we also enjoyed relaxing together too. We would hang out at lunchtimes, usually by going to the firm's canteen. At lunchtime we talked about anything and everything. We often talked about the most important things in life. And then, when we stopped talking about football, sometimes the conversation turned to Jesus!

Everyone in the office knew I was a Christian. As we sat down to eat our food, I would close my eyes and quietly pray a prayer of thanks. Regularly I'd open my eyes to find that while I had my eyes shut, my portion of chips had been transferred to someone else's plate. It happened repeatedly, which was a bit tiresome, but I have to give it to them – it was a swift and skilful manoeuvre, as my eyes weren't closed for that long! Anyway, I recall that story to tell you that while my eyes were closed and I was giving thanks for my food, I also prayed a quick prayer to be able to speak about Jesus. But at the same time, at the very moment I prayed that prayer, in the back of my mind I was thinking, 'I hope someone doesn't ask me to lead them to Christ' because, back then, I wouldn't have known how to do that. And that was just the start of my concerns. I feared that I might be asked searching questions about the reliability of the Bible, or the problem of suffering or the place of other religions. I didn't have a clue how to answer any of those questions.

So there I was, praying every morning, and then again at lunchtime, for opportunities to speak about Jesus, yet, in my heart of hearts, I was desperately hoping that a whole host of issues wouldn't be raised. No wonder I was full of fear. I didn't want to look a chump and I didn't want to blow any opportunity that God might give me, especially as I *did* have the conviction that the gospel was true and that it was crucial that everyone turn to Christ for salvation.

If we're to overcome fear, it is a great help if we gain confidence in knowing how to answer the tough questions that come our way. That's what Peter told his readers:

Always be prepared to give an answer to everyone who asks you to give the reason for the hope that you have (1 Pet. 3:15).

If we know Christ is Lord, we will want to get ready to speak for him. In the next chapter we'll begin to think about how we can get prepared. Before we do, there is, second, another sort of confidence which must undergird our practical preparations to speak.

It is really helpful to gain confidence in how to answer questions but we must not place our confidence in *our* ability to give great answers. Of course, we want to set forth the truth plainly. It is right to work at that. But, however brilliant our answers are, we must not put our confidence in the brilliance (or not!) of our answers. We can have the most theologically astute responses to questions but, without a work of God, our friend will not be converted.

The apostle Paul wrote that it is God who makes:

his light shine in our hearts to give us the light of the knowledge of the glory of God in the face of Christ (2 Cor. 4:6).

This is crucial to remember, otherwise we might be tempted to think that if we just learn how to answer people's questions, then they will always become Christians. Think that way and it won't be long before we find ourselves very disappointed. Our answers alone will be inadequate. However much preparation we do, it takes the miracle of God opening blind eyes for someone to become a Christian. That is God's great work and his alone. That said, we have a part to play. As the apostle Paul wrote:

> we do not preach ourselves, but Jesus Christ as Lord (2 Cor. 4:5).

As we do that, we need to place our confidence in Jesus and not in ourselves. Christ the Lord is a mighty saviour; we can be confident in his power to save.

So, when the conversation turns to the things of Jesus Christ, if we have the three C's of conviction, compassion and confidence all flowing from a genuine fear of the Lord, we might well find the sweaty palms and the racing heart become a thing of the past. We might even find ourselves quite enjoying the chance to speak about Jesus.

Be prepared

Making resolutions is not always a great idea, especially at the turn of the year. As someone said to me years ago, 'January 2nd is the day when it's easier to break a promise than it is to break a habit.' For that reason I made a New Year's resolution a few years ago that I've managed to keep since. I resolved to make no more New Year's resolutions!

However, twenty-seven years ago I made a promise to myself that I have largely kept. This promise has turned out to be a huge help in my personal evangelism. I promised myself that I would never be caught out on the same question twice. I didn't realise it then, but deciding this began a process which has helped me overcome one of the big fears in evangelism – the fear of not knowing what to say.

When I first became a Christian and began to

tell people about Jesus, I found the same questions coming up again and again. And I'd kick myself when I was no better at answering the question the second and third time around than I was the first time I encountered it. I came to the point where I realised that there was no shame in not being able to answer a question I'd never been asked before, but I resolved never to be stumped on any question a second time. From that moment on and to this day, if someone asks me a question about the gospel that I can't answer, I say, 'That's a great question. I don't know the answer but I'll go away and think about it and come back to you.'

This is a much better response than it may seem. It's certainly better than bluffing it. You may know the old adage, 'The secret of success is sincerity. Once you can fake that you've got it made!' That may make us smile, but it's not a great way to live life and it's certainly not a good approach to evangelism! Admitting that I don't have all the answers, and knowing that it's OK to say that, gives me freedom to go away, think about the question and then return to my questioner with a carefully considered answer. Not only does that keep the conversation going, but it also equips me the next time the same question is raised.

Having this approach has, over the years, taken away my fear of not knowing what to say in evangelism. If I don't know the answer, I say so. Then having gone away and thought about how to answer the question, I have a bank of answers tucked away in my mind. Oh, for sure, I still get frustrated with myself when I haven't answered questions clearly. But it is much rarer for me to be completely paralysed by fear. I know that I have at least something to say on most of the questions that people ask. And when our fear starts to evaporate, we don't run and we don't fight. As we noted in the last chapter, the apostle Peter told fearful Christians:

> Always be prepared to give an answer to everyone who asks you to give the reason for the hope that you have. But do this with gentleness and respect. (1 Pet. 3:15)

Getting prepared to answer questions does help our fear evaporate. It helps us to stop running away from gospel opportunities. It helps us not to be aggressive either.

There's still so much I have to learn about sharing

the gospel, but being prepared to answer tough questions chases away that overwhelming fear of not knowing what to say. All I have to do is recall the answers I've thought about. Like me, you may not want to make another New Year's resolution in your life, but providing you're not reading this on January 1st, why not promise yourself that you'll never be caught out on the same question twice?

Take people to Jesus

4

In just one week, I learnt one of the most valuable things I have ever learnt about answering questions. When I was at theological college, I was invited to be part of a university mission, led by a very able evangelist, Paul Weston. Before we went on the mission week, we had a few training sessions in which Paul encouraged us to try and answer any question from the lips of Jesus. I don't think I realised then just how helpful this idea would be.

Similarly, John Stott wrote:

In all evangelism … our chief and overriding responsibility is to point people to Jesus. In every evangelistic proclamation, the wisest evangelist keeps bringing the conversation back to the person and work of Jesus Christ.[1]

---

[1] John Stott, *Through the Bible Through the Year* (Lion Hudson, 2006), p. 299.

The gospel is about Jesus Christ, and so in every evangelistic conversation we should try and take people to Jesus. He is the one we want to talk about. He is the one person that everyone needs to know about. He is the way we know God, the way we come to God and the one in whom we can have life.

So, whenever we're asked a question about what we believe – whatever the question – we'd do well to ask ourselves, 'What did Jesus say on this issue?' or, 'How can I answer this question from the life or lips of Jesus?' Answering a question like this does three things:

1. When I take people to Jesus, I am taking them to the one who is the focus of the gospel.
2. If the questioner doesn't like the answer, their issue is with Jesus, not me.
3. Having spoken about Jesus, it's then very natural to talk more about Jesus as the conversation progresses.

Continuing to point to Jesus is what we want to do. Yes, we want to answer the question put before us. Yet it is even better if we can take the initiative in a conversation and help our friend understand the gospel of Jesus' death for sins and his resurrection as Lord. So, my first principle in answering difficult questions is to take people to Jesus.

Before we go any further, though, let me tell you what I am *not* saying here. I am *not* saying that I think that Jesus' words are more inspired than the rest of the Bible. The whole Bible is inspired. All Scripture is God-breathed. The gospel of grace runs right through the Bible from the first page to the last. The entire Bible is about Jesus – Jesus himself said as much. Answering those who were questioning his testimony, Jesus said:

> You diligently study the Scriptures because you think that by them you possess eternal life. *These are the Scriptures that testify about me,* yet you refuse to come to me to have life. (John 5:39–40, italics mine).

The whole Bible has one unifying theme and Jesus Christ is the focus of its message. Therefore Jesus is the one we want people to be considering in evangelism. And once we've started speaking about Jesus Christ, we're presenting the One who is at the very heart and centre of life.

Take people to the cross

5

I love sport. All sport. Tennis is the game I play most (just in case you hadn't picked that up already) but I love following and watching all sport. In that most English of sports, cricket, there is an expression that has found its way into everyday parlance: 'being on the back foot.' If you google the expression, you'll find definitions along the lines of: 'in a defensive posture; off balance'. To explain, in cricket the batsman will try to get on the front foot to play an attacking shot. When a batsman is on the back foot, they've been bowled a ball that has left them in a bit of bother.

I offer that little cricket lesson because far too often I worry that when Christians are asked questions, we automatically feel that we're on the back foot. We get defensive and feel off balance.

But Peter, who, as we've seen, urges us to be constantly ready to reply to questions, encourages his readers to see it quite differently.

To continue the cricket analogy, he sees a question as an opportunity to get on the front foot and to play a positive stroke.

As we saw in the last chapter, when someone asks me any question, I want to try and answer that question by taking them to the person of Jesus Christ. That is my first principle in answering questions. Head for Jesus at all times, if you possibly can. But then, if I can, I want to get on the front foot and follow up my answer with a (hopefully) penetrating question which takes my friend to the cross. I've tried to illustrate what I mean in this diagram:

So, whenever someone asks me a question, I have three aims:

Figure 1

1. Take them to Jesus.
2. Take the initiative – by asking a good question.
3. Take them to the cross – to explain the gospel.

The second step of asking a question is so very helpful because it can probe, challenge and extend a person's thinking. It can help shape their conclusions. It can also be diagnostic. It can help you understand better where your friend is up to in their own thinking. This can help you know what would be most helpful for you to talk about next. What's more, it can change the tone of a discussion. Asking a question shows that you are interested in what your friend thinks. And you are! It shows that you want to listen to them. Finally, asking a good question can slow the conversation down in a helpful way. It can stop it becoming either a confrontational argument or a one-sided lecture.

But more than all that, asking a question reflects something very important about God. When people came to Jesus with a question, very often he asked them a question too. For example, when an expert in the law asked Jesus, 'what must I do to inherit eternal life?' Jesus replied, 'What is written in the Law? … How do you read it?' (Luke 10:25–26). God has questions to ask every person. We can easily forget this. When someone asks us a question about Jesus, we can be tempted to feel defensive. We can feel as if we are being put in the dock – or that God is being put in the dock. Actually, though, the living God of the Bible is never the one in the dock. No. God has questions – challenging questions – that he wants to ask all men and women. We can reflect something of that truth in the conversations we have with people. So, we need to think of good questions to ask.

When someone asks us a question about Jesus, we can be tempted to feel defensive

The best questions flow on from the answers we have just given. In particular, we need to think of questions which will direct the conversation to the heart of the gospel. We want to be able to take our questioner to the cross and resurrection of Christ. That is my aim as I speak with unbelievers and so it is also my third principle: 'Take people to the cross'. My aim is not to enlarge their general knowledge. I want to show them their need of Christ.

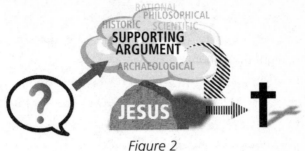

Figure 2

Figure 2 illustrates what I would regularly find myself doing before I began to make a conscious effort to always go to the person of Christ first. I would often turn initially to what we might call a supporting argument. I might cite a piece of archaeological or historical evidence for the reliability of the Bible. Sometimes I would attempt to give a scientific answer to how the world came into existence. At times I'd even attempt a philosophical rationale for the meaning of life.

When I began by turning to such supporting arguments, I found that I regularly came across two problems. First, if I was talking to a scientist or a philosopher, I would quickly find myself out of my depth. Second, having started down that track, it felt like an unnatural crunching of the gears to then try and talk about Jesus (as illustrated by the broken

49

arrow in figure 2). But starting with Jesus as my initial response to any question makes it much easier to talk about him as the conversation progresses.

All that said, in reality conversations rarely go smoothly and in the direction I expect or want them to go (as the ideal scenario of figure 1 depicts). Who of us doesn't know that experience of working out in our minds how an encounter is going to turn out? When I 'play' or 'replay' conversations in my mind, the whole thing goes perfectly. In my mind, I give brilliant answers to every question I'm asked and leave my 'opponent' completely stumped or wowed by my answers. They end up asking me, 'What must I do to be saved?' The whole exchange leaves me looking like the evangelist the world has been waiting for! In my dreams, that's how it plays out. In reality … Well, figure 3 illustrates reality:

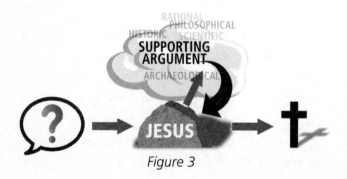

Figure 3

Real-life conversations are 'messy'. No two conversations are the same. The first bit may go the way we expect, because we've rehearsed how to answer that question. But after our first response, the conversation usually gets 'messy' and jumbled.

In my first response to any question I will always try and take people to Jesus, but the next question I'm asked could take us anywhere! My friend might ask me a specific question about something they saw on TV about archaeology, or about the historical accuracy of the New Testament, for example. I might then bring in a supporting argument about that subject, if I know one. Or I might need to say that I don't know but that I will go away and find out and come back to them. But even if the conversation has now moved away from Jesus, it is very much easier to bring the conversation back to him, as Jesus was the first person I mentioned in the conversation. It's very natural to say, 'You know I was talking about Jesus earlier, well …' Figure 3 illustrates what I have just described. This approach has really helped me in my personal evangelism. That's not to say that every conversation I have ends with my questioner asking, 'And what must I do to be saved?' I don't want to leave you with the impression that adopting this approach will result in all those people you've been praying for finally being immediately convinced that Jesus is indeed the saviour of the world.

How God chooses to use what I say is entirely in his hands. But I can say that taking people to Jesus, and then getting on the front foot by asking a good question, has regularly meant that I'm not stumped – and has sometimes kept the scoreboard ticking over. Sorry, that's too many cricket phrases!

Meat on the bones

6

I was 5-0 down in the first set, playing a guy who was fifteen years younger than me, fitter than me and a much better tennis player than me. My prospects already looked bleak and it was highly probable that my hugely imbalanced win/loss record was going to become even more lopsided. Still, fiercely competitive as I am, and never knowing when I'm beaten, I thought to myself, 'I've got to do something to turn this around.' As we changed ends, a few ideas of how to get back into the match sprang to mind, but I swiftly ruled them out as viable options. After all, tripping him up or taking a pair of pliers to his racket strings is hardly becoming conduct for a Christian minister and I'd paid good money to be part of this club!

Lacking any serious options, but wanting to buy

myself some time, all I could manage was to ask my opponent, 'So, what do you do for a living?' He told me he had just finished uni and then he asked me what kept me busy during the day. 'I'm a vicar,' I answered. This is usually a complete conversation stopper, so I was pleasantly surprised when Matt responded with, 'Oh, how do you know God exists?' And there was my opportunity. He was asking me for the Christian evidence for God. What should I have done? If I'd read the last chapter, I would have taken him to Jesus. What *did* I do? Well, it was a beautiful summer's evening, and the trees lining the tennis courts were gently swaying in the warm, pleasant breeze. 'Just look all around you,' I said. 'There's plenty of evidence for God's existence.'

I don't recall exactly how the conversation went from there, but I do remember that we ended up talking about the Big Bang theory (not the American TV sitcom, but the cosmological model for the early development of the universe approximately 13.8 billion years ago). As far as witnessing to the gospel, I wouldn't say that what I said was a complete disaster – the only disaster in my life that day was the embarrassing scoreline at the end of the match. The way I answered Matt's question *wasn't* a complete waste of time, but I really didn't make the most of the opportunity.

In the last chapter, we thought about being prepared to answer questions by taking people to Jesus. Now, in this chapter, I'd like to put some meat on the bones and flesh out how we might do that. So, let's start with the question that Matt asked me on the tennis court on that gorgeous summer's evening.

The evidence for the existence of God is one of those questions that comes up again and again. This is especially the case since the rise of the new atheists in recent years has gained momentum with the publication of books like Richard Dawkins' *The God Delusion*.[2] The question of God's existence is presented in different

The evidence for the existence of God is one of those questions that comes up again and again

ways. Sometimes people ask it straight out, as Matt did. Other times it's delivered as a statement,

---

2 Richard Dawkins, *The God Delusion* (Bantam Books, 2006).

perhaps as 'I can't believe there's a God,' or as, 'I'm not prepared to rip my brains out and flush them down the toilet and completely ignore all the scientific evidence that tells me clearly that there isn't a God.' (Yes, that was actually said to me. Wonderfully, the guy who said it did become a Christian about six months later and he is still going on with the Lord today!)

So, the question comes in different ways, but however and whenever it arrives in a conversation, how can we answer it by taking people to Jesus?

In preparation
Before thinking about what we might say to an unbeliever, let me take you back a step. To be ready to answer that question, we need to ask ourselves, 'What is the Christian answer to how we know that God exists?' We need to think this through, with some prior preparation, before we engage in conversation.

In a nutshell, we know God exists because God himself has revealed himself to us. That is the Christian answer. Theologians call this 'revelation'. The Christian belief for God hasn't come about because Christians arrogantly think that we're exceptionally clever and have worked out that God really is there. Christians are not certain of God's existence as a result of our rational or intellectual ability to reason that God must be there. Our certainty doesn't come from the realm of philosophy. It comes from the fact that God has revealed himself to us.

I am unlikely to use the word 'revelation' when I am talking to people about the existence of God. But right now we're doing our homework, getting prepared to know how to answer the question when it comes to us.

God has revealed himself to us. That's why we're certain of the existence of God. Next we need to think about how God has done that. How has God revealed himself to us? The Bible tells us that God has revealed himself in creation (Ps. 19; Rom. 1:20), so my answer to Matt on the tennis court was not unbiblical. However, God has also revealed himself through his word, speaking to the world through his prophets and the apostles. And most fully and gloriously, God has revealed himself in Christ:

He [Christ] is the image of the invisible God (Col. 1:15).

No-one has ever seen God, but God the One and Only, who is at the Father's side, has made him known (John 1:18).

The self-revelation of God in Christ is the supreme revelation of God. God is revealed much more fully and clearly in Christ than he is in creation. That's why my answer on the tennis court was not the best answer I could have given. And in answering the question by looking at creation, I inadvertently steered the conversation towards the beginning of the world and the Big Bang.

I'd have done much better talking about Jesus, because there is no better revelation of God than Jesus. And I'd have done better talking about Jesus because the gospel is about Jesus (Mark 1:1; Rom. 1:1–3). What's more, I'd have done better talking about Jesus because Matt needed to know about Jesus. And I'd have done better talking about Jesus, because once Jesus was the topic of our discussion, it would have been much easier to direct the conversation towards the cross and the heart of salvation.

In conversation

So much for the theory. What would all this look like in a conversation as I try to answer the question that Matt asked me? How do you know that God exists? In my mind, I am clear that God has revealed himself to us supremely in Jesus Christ. My job now is to present that truth to Matt in a succinct, clear and engaging way.

Oh, and one final thing before I launch in! I need to tell you that I always have a Bible with me. Even on the tennis court, in my tennis bag, I have a small Bible next to my water bottle and my sunglasses. Years ago someone said to me, 'Never go out without a Bible with you – it's the sword of the Spirit, and we're in a battle. Why would you want to go anywhere without your sword?' It's a bit cheesy, but it's stayed with me. And all cheese aside, it really is very helpful to have a Bible in personal evangelism for a number of reasons. Most crucially, when we answer questions from the Bible, we demonstrate that we're not just giving our thoughts and opinions but are pointing to the Bible as our authority.

Now, let me take you back to that warm summer's evening. I'm 5-0 down in the first set. (I don't know why I keep reminding you of that!) As we change ends, as it turned out, to complete the set, I am presented with a brilliant opportunity to tell a young man, just out of uni, why Christians know that God exists. Clearly, I don't have long. We have a match to complete. Although in hindsight, as the court was booked for a full-length tennis match, I had longer than I might have thought! Still, I reckon, in any conversation, I have about three minutes as a first stab to answer a question. If I rabbit on for twenty minutes without drawing breath, even if I manage to give the most brilliant explanation of the gospel ever given in the history of Christianity, the chances are my friend will never ask me another question – never. So, how can I answer the question clearly, faithfully and in an engaging manner, getting right to the heart of the answer in three minutes? With hindsight, a helpful answer would be this:

So, how can I answer the question clearly, faithfully and in an engaging manner, getting right to the heart of the answer in three minutes?

That's a great question. In a nutshell, Christians believe God exists because he has come and shown himself to us. (And this is where I reach into my tennis bag, get out my Bible and turn to Mark 4:35–41). In one of the accounts of Jesus' life, Jesus is in a boat with some of the people who follow him. And we're told that a furious squall came up, and that waves broke over the boat. It was such a bad storm that some of Jesus' followers thought they were going to drown. So they turned to Jesus, who amazingly was asleep in the boat, and they woke him and asked, 'Teacher, don't you care if we drown?' (verse 38).

What happened next is amazing. Jesus didn't go to the back of the boat, grab hold of the tiller and guide them through the storm and into safety. No, Jesus got up, rebuked the wind and said to the waves, 'Be still!' (verse 39). And then the wind died down and it was completely calm. In an instant, the raging sea was as calm as a duck pond. What an extraordinary thing. Jesus' followers asked, 'Who is this? Even the wind and the waves obey him!' (verse 41). And that's the big question: who is this person who can control the wind and waves? Jesus did many other miracles like this. Right throughout his life on earth, Jesus did things that only God can do, to prove that he is God. That's why Christians believe that God exists, because, in Jesus, God came and walked among us to prove that he exists.

Where the conversation goes from there depends on how my questioner responds to what I have said. But even if I say nothing else, I have given an answer that gets right to the nub of the issue. I have left my friend with evidence that God does exist and that we can know about God by looking at the person of Jesus. As I walk away from that discussion, I can pray that the Holy Spirit would take the truth of his word and apply it deep into my friend's heart.

Of course, I would love the conversation to go further. Now, if I can, I want to take them to the cross and the heart of the gospel message. This is where I get on the front foot with a telling question that will lead the way to the cross. The sort of question I have up my sleeve is, 'So, there is good evidence that God came in the person of Jesus and walked among us. But have you ever considered why Jesus might have come to earth?'

My friend may not want to hear any more at this point. But he may! I am praying that he does! And if he does, the conversation is now moving towards the reason Jesus came. So, from his initial question about the existence of God, in no time at all, I am talking about the cross. This is where I want to be, because this is what my friend most needs to know.

So, there's the meat on the bones. It is a worked example of my three principles about answering people's questions: take people to Jesus; take the initiative by asking a penetrating question; and do this in order to take people to the cross. As I've already said, in real life conversations rarely go to plan, but who knows, if I'd spoken of Jesus on that hot summer's evening on the tennis court, our conversation might have led to a result that really counted.

Stay in the water

7

'If at first you don't succeed …' We all know how the saying ends. Perseverance is a great thing in all walks of life. To improve in any area of life we have to keep trying. Behind world-beating, talented sport stars, behind gifted musicians and behind the most successful entrepreneurs in business lies much dedicated hard graft. I imagine you're better at your job now than on your first day at work – because you've had more practice at it. In the last eighteen months I've hit hundreds of tennis balls in an attempt to reshape my backhand, and, as a result, I can now hit a better shot down the line than I ever could before. It's still not brilliant, but at least it doesn't hit the back fence quite so often these days! In all areas of life, practice may not make something perfect, but it does make us more proficient.

> *When we remember a previous 'disaster' in evangelism, that may make us want to flee any prospect of sharing our faith*

It's no different with answering tough evangelistic questions. The problem is that when we've had an embarrassing experience, we may be tempted to shy away from the advice: 'Try, try, try again.' When we remember a previous 'disaster' in evangelism, that may make us want to flee any prospect of sharing our faith. But, please, let me encourage you to keep trying – you will get better at it. Trust me – I'm a vicar!

I once heard the evangelist John Chapman say, 'Evangelism is a lot like swimming; you can't learn to do it if you won't get in the water!' And, of course, we need to *stay* in the water too. We need to keep taking evangelistic opportunities if we want to get better at making the most of them.

Practice won't make us perfect in evangelism. But practice can certainly enable us to say something clear and helpful. And just knowing that we can do that removes some of the fear. When fear is no longer hampering our efforts to tell people about Jesus, we will look for more opportunities *and* we will take them when they come our way.

After some careful research and a bit of practice you might even find yourself looking forward to being asked searching questions about the existence of God, the reliability of the Bible, or the place of other religions. Try, try, try again and you could find yourself moving from being someone who dreads the prospect of being asked to give a reason for the hope you have, to actually looking forward to being presented with challenging questions. You may even find yourself saying, 'Bring it on!'

Let's have another go

8

In chapter 6 we saw one example of answering questions by taking people to Jesus. Now it's just a matter of practice. So let's have a go at another question: 'You get to heaven by being good, don't you?'

As the vicar of a local parish church I often take funerals of people I've never met before. On one occasion, sitting in the front room of a tearful widow who was speaking of her late husband, she said to me, 'He wasn't a religious man, but he was a good man. He's in a better place now, isn't he, vicar?' Hers wasn't the confident, assured statement of a real Christian believer, but here was a dear grieving woman clutching at straws and hoping, beyond hope, that there was something beyond the grave. And her only hope was that being a good, decent, upright citizen was the qualification for entry into God's heaven.

It's a basic misunderstanding that we'll encounter often. The idea that being good gets us to heaven is a misconception about Christianity that is rife in our culture. Most Brits, if they think about these things at all, believe that Christianity is a moral code to live by. With that belief, they assume that at the end of their lives, if they've kept their nose clean, paid their taxes, never been in trouble with the police, and been good, decent citizens, then surely they'll be allowed into heaven. It might come as a question, or a statement, but we will almost certainly encounter this idea as we talk about Jesus Christ: 'You get to heaven by being good, don't you?' So, let's have a go at trying to answer that question, by taking people to Jesus.

In preparation
Once again, before trying to answer the question, we need to do our homework. Why do Christians believe that being good is not good enough for heaven? The answer is not difficult. None of us are good. The theological issue that we are dealing with when tackling this question is the doctrine of sin:

… all have sinned and fall short of the glory of
God (Rom. 3:23).

All of us have become like one who is unclean,
and all our righteous acts are like filthy rags
(Is. 64:6).

In short, the problem is simply this: we are not
good – none of us. We have all failed. We are
sinners. We have done many things that are deeply
offensive to God. We have rejected God, broken
his laws, treated others badly and are thoroughly
selfish, self-centred and self-obsessed. Even our
good deeds are tainted by sin. Theologians call
this 'total depravity'. That's not the belief that
we're as bad as we could possibly be, but is the
understanding that even the good things we do
are corrupt. We don't act from right motives. We
don't do good for the glory of God.

So when answering the question of why 'good'
people don't go to heaven, we need to demonstrate,
to those who think that they are good, that people
are *not* good. It is the utter sinfulness of all human

beings that we are trying to get across. For anyone to grasp the implications of this for their lives, they need to have much more than an intellectual grasp of what we're saying. We need the Holy Spirit to deeply convict people that they are sinners and that they don't deserve heaven.

So, the answer's not difficult. We could just say it baldly: 'The Bible says we are all sinful and don't deserve heaven.' Put like that, we would be telling the truth, but it's not much of an explanation and it doesn't really engage the heart. Taking people to Jesus and allowing him to answer the question will be far more winsome, and if those we talk to don't like what they hear, their issue is with Jesus! Most importantly, by steering the conversation in the direction of Jesus, we're heading towards the person who is the only solution to the problem of our sinfulness.

In conversation

A kindly man in his sixties once said to me, 'I'm not religious, but I always try my hardest. I've never done anyone any harm.' I could have responded sarcastically: 'You *always* try your hardest? You've *never* done *anyone* any harm? What a remarkable person you are. What a privilege it is for me to meet you!'

That might have sounded clever, but a cutting reply like that doesn't begin to display the compassion for lost sheep that Jesus demonstrated. It's no surprise to learn that Jesus didn't respond like that when a man, who believed he had lived a good life, asked Jesus about getting into heaven. I'm thinking of the rich man who ran up to Jesus and asked him:

Good teacher … what must I do to inherit eternal life? (Mark 10:17).

That's the story I turn to whenever I'm asked this big question about whether good people get to heaven. The rich man is asking how he can get to heaven – 'what must I do to inherit eternal life?' – and, as the story unfolds, we discover that he thinks he is a good person.

It may be that someone asks me, 'Why do you think that only Christians go to heaven?' Or somebody may make a statement such as, 'All good people go to heaven, don't they?' However the subject is raised, I then get out my Bible and turn to Mark 10:17–31 and say something like this:

That is such an important question. Many people think that Christianity is about trying to live a good moral life. That's why I find an incident recorded in one of the accounts of Jesus' life so fascinating. You'll see here in verse 17 that a young man ran up to Jesus and asked him, 'Good teacher … what must I do to inherit eternal life?'

What I find so fascinating about this conversation is what Jesus said next. He said, 'Why do you call me good? … No-one is good – except God alone' (verse 18). There's our problem. We think we're good, but Jesus says that only God is good. We're not good, and Jesus showed this man that no-one is good by talking about the Ten Commandments. Jesus asked, 'You know the commandments: "Do not murder, do not commit adultery, do not steal, do not give false testimony, do not defraud, honour your father and mother."' And the man replied, 'Teacher … all these I have kept since I was a boy' (verses 19–20).

The man thought he was a good person. In his mind, he thought he'd kept the Ten Commandments. But what I find surprising here is that while Jesus quoted the commandments, he didn't cite all ten. So, the young man, who was a Jewish lad and would have been steeped in the Jewish law, should have said to Jesus, 'Hang on a moment, Jesus, you've missed out some of the commandments.' And then the penny should have dropped. Jesus had left out the first four commandments about our attitude to God, including those that tell us not to put other things before God and not to have idols in our lives. If the young man had stopped and thought about the Ten Commandments, he'd have realised that he had fallen at the first hurdle – he didn't love God above all things.

When we're honest with ourselves, we know that we don't keep God's commandments either. We too have broken God's law, at many levels. We don't love God with all our heart, soul, mind and strength, and we don't love other people as we should. To help this young man to realise that he wasn't a good person, Jesus said to him, 'Go, sell everything you have and give to the poor, and you will have treasure in heaven. Then come, follow me' (verse 21). The man went away sad. He didn't do as Jesus said. Money was more important to him than God. This young man had put wealth and riches before the living God and made money his god. For us, it may not be money that we worship, but if we look honestly at our lives, we have to admit that we've put other things before God. We push God out to the margins of our lives. We have sidelined the God who has given us every breath we take. So, Jesus says, we're not good and we don't deserve heaven.

At this point I've answered the question. Good people don't go to heaven because none of us are good. But there's so much more I want to say. All I've done so far is given the bad news. I still have the momentous news of the gospel to tell. I want to speak about how Jesus died on a cross so that bad people can go to heaven. But this is a conversation I'm having, so I need to draw breath and give my questioner a chance to respond. What they say next will determine where the conversation goes from here. However, if they've been listening to me at all, then I expect their next question to be something about being good, or about God's commandments, or about Jesus. And even if this doesn't happen, it should be easy to bring the conversation back to the big and crucial issue of our sinfulness (without ever needing to use that word).

So, I've taken my questioner to Jesus. The next thing I want to do is to take the initiative with a good question and to take the conversation to the cross. So when (and if) that's appropriate, I can ask a penetrating question, like, 'Have you ever considered how Jesus can deal with the problem of us not being good enough for heaven?'

I was asked this very question about being good enough for heaven while I was on a train journey. I was reading my Bible and the young man opposite me asked if I was a Christian. He wasn't a Christian himself, but he had Christian friends from his days at Exeter University and he'd clearly engaged with the gospel. So I asked him, 'What's the big stumbling block for you when it comes to the Christian faith? Or, if I may put it another way, if you could ask God one question and you knew he would answer it, what would it be?' And without hesitating he said, 'Oh that's easy. I don't understand why God doesn't let good people into heaven.'

So I turned to Mark chapter 10 and we looked at the encounter between Jesus and the rich man. That was the day I learnt the importance of trying to answer a question in three minutes.

Only a few minutes after we'd looked at the Bible, the train pulled into Leicester station and a businesswoman in the seat next to me got off the train. I hadn't realised that she was getting off at the next stop, but I was aware that while I was talking to the young man opposite me, she was listening in to the whole conversation. I don't know if the young man was convinced by my answer – we had a good and stimulating conversation for sure. I don't have a clue whether the businesswoman understood anything of what I said that day. But I do know that a concise answer meant that she had heard, from the lips of Jesus, why she isn't good enough for heaven. And while she got off at Leicester, who knows if overhearing our conversation led to her getting on the right track!

Just get me started

9

I've always found threading a needle difficult. When I was a boy, I simply didn't have the dexterity to do it. Now that I'm older, I can't see well enough to do it. So whenever I've needed to do any sewing (which thankfully isn't that often), before I can get started I need someone to thread the needle for me. I need someone to get me started.

You may feel that way about the things we've thought about so far in this book. You may be keen to adopt this approach to answering questions, but you're still not sure how to put it into practice. As I mentioned before, at some point you'll just have to jump in and have a go – just us you need to actually get in the pool if you want to learn to swim. But I understand that before you dive in the deep end, having a few more examples could be very helpful. So, in this chapter, I want to give you brief outlines for a number of the most common questions people ask to get you started. This chapter is not like chapters 6 and 8. I'm not going to give you a full-blown, step-by-step breakdown of my thinking, followed by a complete answer. No, here I'll lay out a few skeleton outlines – and then you'll have to put the meat on the bones yourself. Why not get together with a Christian friend to think about how you might do that?

Before we look at some outlines, please know that these are only suggestions. In time you'll be able to think of other ways to answer the questions that come your way. You'll find ways that suit you better. So don't feel that these are the only ways to answer any given question. I really don't want to put you in an evangelistic straitjacket. All I'm doing here is threading the needle for you, so that you can get started.

I'll begin with the question we considered in chapter 6, so that you can refer back to that chapter and see how this outline can be turned into a succinct three-minute answer.

1. How do you know God exists?

In preparation – working out the issue

- ■ Christians believe that God has revealed himself.
- ■ The issue is revelation.
- ■ God has revealed himself through creation (Ps. 19; Rom. 1:20); through his word (the prophets and the apostles); but supremely in his Son (John 1:18; Col. 1:15).

In conversation – taking people to Jesus

- ■ Bible passage: Mark 4:35–41.
- ■ The disciples were terrified in a storm. Jesus stilled the storm with just a word. Verse 41 asks the question we need to answer: 'Who is this?' The Bible answers that question. The one who can make the waves still is the Lord Almighty (see Ps. 89:9).

Taking the initiative – asking a question to lead towards the cross

'So God has come and walked among us, and demonstrated that he is God by the remarkable things that he did. Have you ever considered why God would come to earth?'

Top tip

Apart from thinking about a penetrating question to take people to the cross, I try to think of a way I might further reinforce my answer. Psalm 89:5–9 are terrific verses to turn to after looking at Mark chapter 4 because they show that only the Lord God Almighty can still storms. For this reason I have often turned to Mark 4:35–41 and then Psalm 89:5–9 when Jehovah's Witnesses have knocked on my door. You might find it useful, before reading on, to look back to chapter 6 and see those steps fleshed out.

2. How can I trust the Bible?

In preparation – working out the issue

- The Bible's words are written by men but also 'breathed out' by God.
- The issue is authorship and inspiration.
- The Bible is God's word and so it is trustworthy and authoritative.

In conversation – taking people to Jesus

- Bible passage: Matthew 5:17–19.
- Jesus believes that the whole Bible has total authority. The phrase 'the Law and Prophets' is shorthand for the entire Old Testament. Jesus believes that not just every word but every punctuation mark is to be believed.

Or:

- Bible passages: John 14:25–26 and John 16:12–13.
- Jesus taught his disciples that the Holy Spirit would remind them of his teaching and enable them to write down his teaching accurately. This gives us confidence that the New Testament is not just the words and thoughts of people but is also inspired by God (as is true of the entire Bible).

Taking the initiative – asking a question to lead towards the cross
'So Jesus has great confidence in the Bible. Have you ever considered what the Bible is about?'

Top tip
I have two distinct passages to turn to whenever I am asked this question, depending on whether my questioner is primarily concerned about the reliability of the Old or New Testament.

3. What about other religions?
In preparation – working out the issue
- Jesus Christ is the unique revelation of God and the solution for sin.
- The issue is the uniqueness of Christ and the problem of sin.

- How is Christianity different to other religions? Other religions are about trying to work our way to God. We will never be able to do this. Jesus Christ is God and he died to bring us to the Father.

In conversation – taking people to Jesus
- Bible passage: John 3:1–10.
- Nicodemus was a very devout member of another religion – Judaism. He approached Jesus to ask him some questions. Jesus told him that, as Nicodemus was, he would not see the kingdom of God. Religion will never get anyone to God. Everyone needs the fresh start that only Jesus can give.

Taking the initiative – asking a question to lead towards the cross
'Jesus' conversation with Nicodemus shows us that religion won't get us right with God. Do you know why Jesus came and why he is different to religion?'

Top tip
I like this passage because without having to leave John chapter 3, I can take people to verse 16 to explain the cross and to verse 36 to present the

eternal decision that everyone must face.

4. Hasn't science disproved Christianity?
In preparation – working out the issue

■ Christianity is about a historical person, Jesus Christ (Mark 1:1).

■ The historical existence of Jesus Christ is not in question.

■ We investigate history by looking at the evidence of eyewitnesses.

■ With this question, people are usually looking for good and solid evidence for why Christians believe what we do.

In conversation – taking people to Jesus

■ Bible passage: John 20:30–31.

■ In John's gospel we are given eyewitness evidence for Jesus being the divine Son of God. We can check out the historical evidence that John gives us. If this is true, then we know that Jesus is God.

Taking the initiative – asking a question to lead towards the cross
'So, have you ever considered the historical evidence for Jesus and what he came to do?'

Top tip

Answer the question that a person has actually asked, not the question you think they will ask next. So, in this example, point out that science hasn't disproved Christianity because Christianity is about the historical person of Jesus. Demonstrate that and then get on the front foot by asking a penetrating question that will take the conversation towards the cross. The evangelistic efforts of many Christians are blunted because they answer a question that hasn't yet been asked and may never be asked. So they end up putting into the questioner's mind issues they don't actually have. Or they make their answer too long and involved because they are trying to answer an anticipated follow-on question, rather than concentrating on the actual question raised.

I hope those outlines get you started. As I said, they are not the only ways to answer these questions. Indeed, as you begin to start thinking along these lines, when you read your Bible and especially as you read the gospels, you'll discover countless ways to answer the questions that people present to you.

Before we turn to the last chapter, it's worth us

considering a few more things about the questions people raise.

What's the question?

First, keep in mind that apologetic issues come in different forms. As I mentioned before, sometimes they come in the form of a question, but at other times they are presented as a statement. So I have been asked, 'How do you know God exists?' And it has been said to me, 'There's no way I can believe there is a God.' The same issue is at the heart of both, but it is presented in different ways and we need to be prepared to 'hear' the questions which a statement is raising.

Does the question need clarifying?

Second, bear in mind that sometimes, before you leap in with an answer, you need to ask a question of clarification to establish what is behind the question put to you. For example, 'I can't believe in a good God who allows suffering' is either a question about the existence of God, or is about the character of God (or both). So, whenever I'm asked that question, I simply reply, 'Tell me more.' I also ask that question because I want to find out if this is an intellectual question or a personal question. A friend of mine says, 'There are armchair sufferers and wheelchair sufferers.' By that he means that there are people who watch the news and are bothered about suffering, but they're not personally suffering and they don't know anyone who's personally suffering. For them, the question is still a real question, but it's an intellectual question. For others, though, they, or someone close to them, are suffering in one way or another. For such a person, this question is deeply personal. The content of the answers we give will be basically the same but the tone of the discussion may need to be very different in different situations. For example, the way we talk to a philosophy student who is intellectually tickled by the issue of suffering will be quite different from the way we talk to someone who is in the midst of great suffering in their own life. Remember that the way we answer questions matters. Show the compassion of Jesus by answering questions patiently and carefully and with love.

While we're dealing with the question of suffering, you might find it useful to know that before I attempt to answer anything relating to this, I always give a few caveats. I point out, 'The question of suffering is a huge issue and it's not going to be answered in a few minutes.' I say that because of all the questions we're presented with, this is potentially the one that people feel most acutely. I continue, 'You're clearly a thoughtful person and if this could be answered quickly and easily, you'd have worked out the answer already.' I usually carry on, 'This issue has flummoxed the greatest minds in history. So there's no easy answer. That said, there are pages and pages in the Bible engaging with the problem of suffering and Jesus himself has much to say on it.' By starting like this, it shows people that my first engagement with the question is not all there is to say on the matter.

Affirm the question

Finally, before answering any question, try to say something that is affirming. 'That's a really good question' or 'That's such an important thing to consider' demonstrates that we are going to take the question seriously. It also gives people confidence to ask more questions as our relationship develops. Of course, we want to be honest, and sometimes the question is not that important or good. Then say something like, 'That's interesting' or 'I've never been asked that before' to show that you have engaged with the question.

I often ask people, 'If you could ask God one question and you knew it would be answered, what would it be?' I have had some bizarre replies, such as, 'Is Elvis dead?' and 'What will the lottery numbers be on Saturday?' But even presented with those sorts of questions, if you are prepared there's a way of engaging with them that gets the conversation onto a serious footing. If anyone ever asks me about Elvis again, I'll say, 'So that question assumes that God knows everything about every human being on this planet – your question assumes that God knows all things. Is that what you think about God?' Similarly, the second time I was asked about the lotto numbers, because I had kept my promise to myself never to be stumped on the same question twice, I responded with, 'That question assumes that God knows everything in advance of it happening, or that God is in control of even the lottery balls. Either way, it says that God is very powerful. Is that what you think about God?' It's not quite taking people to the lips or person of Jesus, but at least we were talking about the character of God.

There are, of course, other questions people ask that we could look at, but hopefully this chapter has gone some way to threading the needle for you so that you can get *sowing*. (And yes, that spelling is deliberate – yes, I am mixing my metaphors, and yes, that is very cheesy!)

Last, but not least

10

In the past few years, I've been given the opportunity to teach the approach laid out in this little book to answering questions people ask about Christianity. As I've encouraged others to take people to Jesus, ask a good question and take people to the cross, I've received some helpful feedback – hence this book. But I think I've often failed to make this last but not least of all points. Or I've not made this last point clearly enough. And it is this: answering tough questions, and indeed all evangelism, is about more – so much more – than being well prepared. It's not just an intellectual issue – it's a spiritual issue. We've considered this a bit already, but I want to stress this to you again before we finish.

Yes, we must be prepared. We've heard that from the apostle Peter. And the apostle Paul tells us that we have a responsibility to preach Christ clearly, as we saw in chapter 2:

> The god of this age has blinded the minds of unbelievers, so that they cannot see the light of the gospel of the glory of Christ, who is the image of God. For we do not preach ourselves, but Jesus Christ as Lord, and ourselves as your servants for Jesus' sake (2 Cor. 4:4–5).

People are blinded by the evil one. They can't see who Jesus is. Our task is to present Christ clearly, by setting forth the truth plainly (2 Cor. 4:2). We must work hard to be clear. We have been given the responsibility to present the truth about Jesus as plainly and clearly as we can. That's what most of this book is about. But no-one is converted by a clear presentation alone:

> God, who said, 'Let light shine out of darkness,' made his light shine in our hearts to give us the light of the knowledge of the glory of God in the face of Christ (2 Cor. 4:6).

It is only when God opens blind eyes and makes the light of the gospel shine into hearts that people see who Jesus is. So we must pray.

Pray for the Holy Spirit to open blind eyes

Are you a praying person? I don't suppose you feel you pray enough – I have yet to meet any Christian who thinks that they pray as much as they should. But let me encourage you to be praying often and regularly – dare I say daily – for unbelievers to be converted. Pray for your unbelieving family, friends, neighbours and colleagues. For this reason many people find a prayer diary helpful. It doesn't need to be elaborate but can be just a list of people and situations to pray for. One list could include all those you know who aren't yet Christians.

Caroline, my wife, went to a day conference a few years back at which Rebecca Manley Pippert was the main speaker. When Caroline returned, I asked her what had most struck her. It was something that Rebecca had said that had most resonated with her. Rebecca prays that the Lord would put across her path people who are open to the gospel. It's a prayer I've prayed often since that day.

Pray for yourself

Next let me encourage you to pray for yourself. Pray that you would set apart Christ as Lord in your heart every day. Pray that you would fear God more than the opinions of those around you. Pray that you would become a better personal evangelist, who increasingly would want to tell people about Jesus Christ. Pray that you would love people more, growing in compassion for the lost, as Jesus had compassion when he saw the crowds. Pray that you would have conviction that the gospel is true and that Christ is a great saviour and a loving Lord. Pray that God would help you as you work hard in preparing to answer the questions that come your way. Pray that he would help you clearly present Christ's powerful gospel.

Keep praying

Pray too after you've had a conversation with someone about the gospel. Whether you have spoken to someone at work whom you see every week day or you have just had a chance encounter with someone on the train, once the conversation has ended, go on praying. You have sown the seed of the word of God. Pray that this seed would grow. The Holy Spirit continues to work in people's lives long after you have left their presence. On the last day we will fully see what God has done with our attempts to speak out for him. We might just find ourselves wonderfully surprised that more of a harvest was produced through the seed that we sowed than we ever imagined.

As I write the news is full of Christians being killed in Iraq at the hands of IS – the, so-called, Islamic State. I have been amazed by the courage of brothers and sisters in Christ who won't convert to Islam. I wonder how they can stand firm when faced with such a fearsome enemy. I guess it begins with having Christ as Lord. I am inspired by people like that all over the world and all throughout history – people who have stood firm even when their lives are in danger. It is a spur to me to be prepared to stand up for Jesus in our culture, where the worst that is likely to happen is to lose a friend, lose face or lose a job.

Don't let fear paralyse you. Rather, as we've seen repeatedly:

But in your hearts set apart Christ as Lord. Always be prepared to give an answer to everyone who asks you to give the reason for the hope that you have. But do this with gentleness and respect (1 Pet. 3:15).

TRUTHFORLIFE®

THE BIBLE-TEACHING MINISTRY OF **ALISTAIR BEGG**

The mission of Truth For Life is to teach the Bible with clarity and relevance so that unbelievers will be converted, believers will be established, and local churches will be strengthened.

Daily Program

Each day, Truth For Life distributes the Bible teaching of Alistair Begg across the U.S., in selected cities in Canada, and in several locations outside of the U.S. on over 1,700 radio outlets. To find a radio station near you, visit *truthforlife.org/station-finder.*

Free Teaching

The daily program, and Truth For Life's entire teaching archive of over 2,000 Bible-teaching messages, can be accessed for free online and through Truth For Life's full-feature mobile app. A daily app is also available that provides direct access to the daily message and daily devotional. Download the free mobile apps at *truthforlife.org/app* and listen free online at *truthforlife.org.*

At-Cost Resources

Books and full-length teaching from Alistair Begg on CD, DVD and MP3CD are available for purchase *at cost, with no mark up.* Visit *truthforlife.org/store.*

Where To Begin?

If you're new to Truth For Life and would like to know where to begin listening and learning, find starting point suggestions at *truthforlife.org/firststep.* For a full list of ways to connect with Truth For Life, visit *truthforlife.org/subscribe.*

Contact Truth For Life

P.O. Box 398000 Cleveland, Ohio 44139
phone 1 (888) 588-7884   **email** letters@truthforlife.org
 /truthforlife   @truthforlife   truthforlife.org

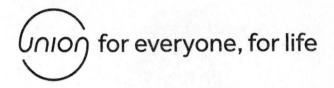 for everyone, for life

If you like what you've read here, check out our website and app. www.uniontheology.org is filled with free, quality resources to bless you.

Our vision is to see the evangelisation of Europe through the raising up of church leaders. To achieve this, our mission under God is to educate and equip pastors, missionaries, church-planters and church-leaders across the continent.

Union offers an affordable, flexible, accessible option for formal theological education.

To find out more, visit:
www.uniontheology.org/courses

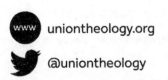
uniontheology.org

@uniontheology

10Publishing is the publishing house of **10ofThose**.

It is committed to producing quality Christian resources that are biblical and accessible.

www.10ofthose.com is our online retail arm selling thousands of quality books at discounted prices. We also service many church bookstalls and can help your church to set up a bookstall. Single and bulk purchases welcome.

For information contact: **sales@10ofthose.com**

or check out our website: **www.10ofthose.com**